THE BRITANNICA COMMON CORE LIBRARY

WHAT IS A

Myth?

GEOFF BARKER

Britannica®
Educational Publishing

IN ASSOCIATION WITH

ROSEN
EDUCATIONAL SERVICES

Published in 2014 by Britannica Educational Publishing (a trademark of Encyclopædia Britannica, Inc.) in association with The Rosen Publishing Group, Inc.
29 East 21st Street, New York, NY 10010

Distributed exclusively by Rosen Publishing.
To see additional Britannica Educational Publishing titles, go to rosenpublishing.com

First Edition

<u>Britannica Educational Publishing</u>
J.E. Luebering: Director, Core Reference Group
Anthony L. Green: Editor, Compton's by Britannica

<u>Rosen Publishing</u>
Hope Lourie Killcoyne: Executive Editor
Nelson Sá: Art Director

Library of Congress Cataloging-in-Publication Data

Barker, Geoff, 1963-
What is a Myth? / Geoff Barker. — First Edition.
    pages cm. — (The Britannica Common Core Library)
Includes bibliographical references and index.
ISBN 978-1-62275-195-2 (library binding) — ISBN 978-1-62275-198-3 (pbk.) — ISBN 978-1-62275-199-0 (6-pack)
1. Mythology—Juvenile literature. I. Title.
BL312.B375 2014
398.2—dc23

2013022570

Manufactured in the United States of America.

Photo credits
Cover: Istockphoto: Fikretozk fg; Shutterstock: Shukaylova Zinaida bg. Inside: Dreamstime: Mg1408 22, Ungorf 28–29, Yamatohd 26–27; Istockphoto: Fikretozk 1fg; Shutterstock: BMJ 14–15, Dan Breckwoldt 20–21, Diez artwork 9, Sergii Figurnyi 23, Michael Hero 8, Kamira 7, Nattika 25, Andrei Nekrassov 6, 16, Marci Paravia 18, Jason Patrick Ross 4, Jose Ignacio Soto 19, SSSCCC 17, Ollie Taylor 10, Topora 24, Gary J. Toth 13, Wavebreakmedia 5, Igor Zh. 12, Shukaylova Zinaida 1bg.

What Is a Myth?

In ancient times, myths were used to explain how the world came to be and how things worked. They were also used to teach lessons or values, and to explain religious beliefs.

Mythical stories gave information, but they were also fun. Listeners were captivated by tales of heroes defeating giants, winged creatures changing into humans, and beautiful women saving men they loved.

Myths were used to explain things in the natural world, such as lightning.

Today, we read myths in books.

Parents told myths to their children, and they passed them on to their own children through many generations. Eventually people started to write down myths.

Myth comes from the Greek word *"mythos,"* which means speech or something spoken. **Generations** means people born at around the same time.

Why Are Myths Told?

Myths have a purpose. Some ask difficult questions such as "where are we from?" and "what happens when we die?" Some myths teach a moral—a lesson you learn.

Characters in myths deal with strong feelings, such as fear and love.

As myths have been told over time, they have changed. Today, there are different versions of the same myth.

The marks on this rock are called runes. They are writings of the Norse people of northern Europe, who told myths.

Many places around the world, from North America to India and China, have similar myths. The stories are not exactly the same, but parts of them are alike.

STORYTELLERS

The ancient Greek poet Homer was a great storyteller. He wrote two mythical poems called the *Iliad* and the *Odyssey*.

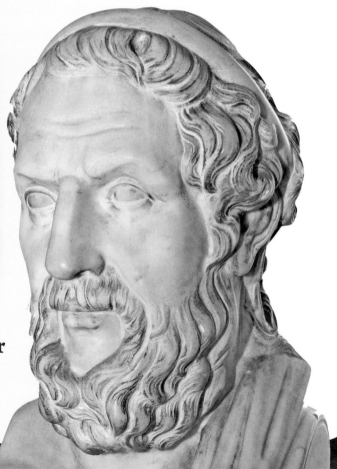

Homer

Themes in Myths

There are many different themes in myths. Creation myths explain how the world began. In some myths, people make difficult decisions as they try to do the right thing. In other myths, heroes fight battles, face incredible creatures, or try to win their sweetheart's love. Some heroes even take on the gods.

In Indian mythology, the great god Brahma the Creator was born from a lotus flower.

Heroes often have awesome adventures. For example, a Greek myth tells of Perseus who chopped off the head of a scary creature named Medusa.

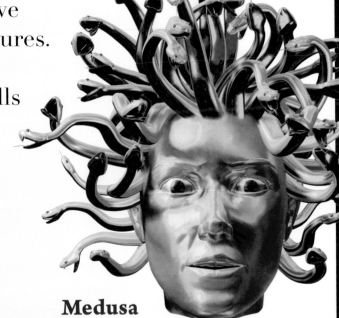

Medusa

STORYTELLERS

The Roman poet Ovid told the tale of Perseus and Medusa. Medusa had live snakes for hair and could turn men to stone with just one look!

Myths Retold

Now that we know what myths are and why they are told, let's read and compare some wonderful myths from around the world.

Ymir, the Frost Giant

This myth is from northern Europe.

In the beginning there was nothing. Then, two places formed. Muspelheim was a world of fire and

Norse people came from the cold northern European countries now known as Iceland, Norway, Sweden, Finland, and Denmark.

Niflheim was a world of ice. Between the two worlds, ice melted and formed Ymir, the Frost Giant.

Three Norse sky gods, Odin, Vili, and Ve, were the creator gods. They killed Ymir and used his body to make Earth. They used his bones as mountains, and his blood to **create** the oceans, lakes, and rivers. Ymir's skull became the sky. The gods threw bright sparks from Muspelheim into the sky to make the sun, moon, and stars.

Finally, the gods created Ask, the first man, and the first woman, Embla.

Compare means to look at two or more things to see how alike or different they are. **Create** means to make something.

Raven

This myth was first told by the Native Americans.

Raven is a trickster and a **shape-shifter***. He hated the never-ending dark. To steal the light, Raven changed into the grandson of the sky chief.*

The Raven myth explains how the stars, moon, and sun were created.

Raven persuaded the sky chief to let him play with the stars, which were hidden in a box. Raven threw the stars into the sky, where they became stuck. Raven cried, so the sky chief gave him another box to keep him happy. This time, Raven took out the moon. He bounced it until it reached the sky. The sun was in the third box. Raven changed back into a bird, and with the sun in his beak, he flew up into the sky, lighting up the world.

A **shape-shifter** is something that can change shape to become something else.

13

Let's Compare

Both *Ymir, the Frost Giant* and *Raven* are myths about the creation of the world.

The Norse myth explains how the world began with the death of Ymir. It also explains the differences between ice and fire. This was important to Norse people because they lived in lands that had glaciers and volcanoes.

> **Glaciers** are huge sheets of slowly-moving ice.
> **Volcanoes** are structures that contain hot, liquid rock. They can explode, or erupt.

The Native American myth explains how the world was created when Raven took the stars, moon, and sun into the sky. Unlike Ymir, Raven was not killed. He was able to outwit the sky chief and tricked him into letting Raven play with the stars, the moon, and the sun. Raven also turned back into his original form. He was a smart being who knew how to get his own way. Raven is an important character in many Native American creation myths.

In Norse myths, the eagle's flapping wings made the winds.

Theseus and the Minotaur

This myth comes from ancient Greece.

Seven boys and seven girls were sent from Athens in Greece to face the Minotaur. The Minotaur lived in a **maze** *on the island of Crete. The Minotaur was half man, half bull, and had a taste for human flesh. Theseus, the son of King Aegeus, asked to go to Crete to fight the beast.*

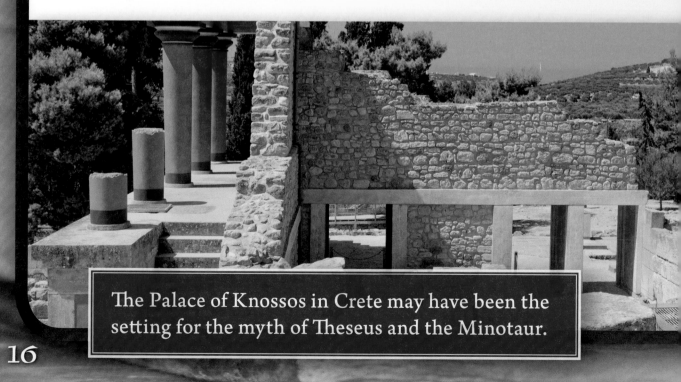

The Palace of Knossos in Crete may have been the setting for the myth of Theseus and the Minotaur.

The king of Crete's daughter, Ariadne, fell in love with Theseus. She gave him a sword to fight the Minotaur and a ball of thread to mark his way in the maze. When Theseus found the Minotaur, he cut off its head. He followed the thread back through the maze to the entrance. Theseus had killed the beast and escaped!

Maze

A **maze** is a winding pathway that leads to many dead ends, with only one exit.

Horus and Seth

This myth comes from ancient Egypt.

Seth killed his brother, King Osiris, and made himself king in place of Osiris's son, Horus. Horus then challenged his uncle to various battles.

The final battle was a boat race. Seth wanted to make both boats from stone, but Horus tricked him. He used a wooden boat that was painted as if it were made of stone. Seth's boat sank and he lost the battle.

Angry that Horus had tricked him, Seth changed himself into a hippopotamus and overturned Horus's boat. Horus was unharmed.

The gods were watching this great battle. They realized that Horus was a worthy king and winner of the contests. Seth was forced to leave the country forever and Horus became king.

Ancient Egyptian kings were made into mummies to preserve them. They were placed in decorated coffins.

Let's Compare

Theseus and the Minotaur and *Horus and Seth* are myths about heroes who do the right thing.

In the Greek myth, Theseus is a hero who offers to fight the Minotaur. By sacrificing himself, Theseus has done the right thing.

In the Egyptian coming-of-age myth, Horus is a hero who knows that he has a duty to kill his uncle, Seth. It is a matter of honor. By fighting Seth, Horus could replace him as king, or pharaoh, and rule Egypt fairly.

A **pharaoh** was an ancient Egptian king whom the Egyptians believed had the powers of a god.

Theseus's adventure in Crete does not last long. He kills the Minotaur and leaves for home in victory. However, Horus's battles with his uncle last for years. They start when he is a young man and continue until Horus finally defeats his uncle.

The ancient Egyptians often buried their pharaohs in huge tombs called pyramids.

Aeneas

This myth comes from ancient Rome.

Aeneas was a great Trojan warrior, but he could not help the Trojans win their war against the ancient Greeks. He knew he had to take his people on a journey to found a new nation.

The ancient Greeks attacked Troy. They tricked the Trojans into letting them into the city of Troy by hiding in a giant wooden horse that they offered to the Trojans as a gift.

Aeneas traveled to the Underworld. There the Sibyl, a prophetess, showed him what a city named Rome would look like in the future. Aeneas then knew that he had to carry on and start the city of Roman people.

This is the city of Rome. A great Roman myth is that Aeneas was the first Roman.

Monkey

Monkey is a popular hero in ancient Chinese myths.

Monkey upset the gods, so he was sent to Hell. He freed himself and looked at the book of judgments. He read that he would live for 342 years. Monkey wanted to live forever, so he crossed out his name.

The Jade Emperor sent Monkey to Heaven so the Emperor could watch over him. There, Monkey looked after the garden where the Peaches of **Immortality** *grew.*

In Chinese myths, the Buddha is wise enough to be able to outwit the lively Monkey trickster.

Monkey stole the Peaches and decided to take over Heaven. The Jade Emperor went to the Buddha for advice. The Buddha held Monkey in his hand and asked him to show his great power. Monkey jumped as far as he could, but realized that he had jumped only across the Buddha's palm. His powers were not so great after all.

Immortality means never dying and living forever.

In Chinese mythology, the Peaches of Immortality could help you to live a long life.

25

Let's Compare

Aeneas and *Monkey* are both myths about character and the right way to behave.

Aeneas is fearless in battle, fighting bravely for the Trojan people. He has to go on an important journey to fulfill his destiny. The Romans see Aeneas as a very important person who found their city.

In the Aeneas myth, the god of winds, Aeolus, created a terrible storm to wreck Aeneas' ship.

Monkey is an unusual character. He is mischievous and enjoys causing trouble. Unlike Aeneas, who is a team player, Monkey is very selfish. Monkey is ambitious, and fights against his destiny. Monkey has to be taught a lesson by the gods, and eventually he becomes wiser. He stands up to authority and power. This popular tale also shows how the Buddha is much wiser than Monkey.

STORYTELLERS

Many people think that the story of Monkey was first written by a writer named by Wu Cheng'en.

Write Your Own Myth

Are you ready to write your own myth? Here are some simple steps to help you start:

1. Pick your setting: Decide where you will set your myth—for example, will it be on a hot desert island or on a strange, distant planet?

2. Choose the main event: Most myths have a central event, such as a terrible storm or a superhuman act. What will *your* myth include?

A fierce dragon could be a character in your myth.

3. Research your myth: Find out as many facts as you can before you write your myth.

4. Pick characters: Decide who your characters will be and what type of people or creatures they are.

5. Sketch your myth: Make a "map" of your myth showing the start, middle, and end.

6. Write and rewrite! Write your myth, then read it through and change anything you do not like.

Finished? Read your myth to a friend, or a family member. Send it in an e-mail to your teacher or a member of your family. You could even post it onto your family's website or blog.

GLOSSARY

advice Information on how to do something.

ambitious Wanting to do really well, or gain power.

authority The power to be in charge.

book of judgments A book that is supposed to show how long we all shall live.

Buddha A religious leader who is the founder of Buddhism.

challenged Set a task, or questioned someone.

creator gods Gods who are believed to have made the world and/or the first people.

defeating Beating someone.

destiny Fate; something that will happen in the future.

duty A task that you are expected to do.

found To create a place.

fulfill To carry out.

honor A sense of the right thing to do.

moral A special teaching or lesson.

mythology Kinds of myth.

nation A country.

original form The way something looked in the beginning.

outwit To get the better of someone by being smart.

prophetess A woman who tells the future.

Sibyl A female prophet (someone who predicts the future).

trickster One who tricks others, often using magical powerls to do so. Tricksters are characters found in oral traditions worldwide.

Underworld The place where the spirits of the dead were thought to live.

values Things that are thought to be important or useful.

victory A win.

warrior A fighter.

worthy Deserving.

Books

Alexander, Heather. *A Child's Introduction to Greek Mythology: The Stories of the Gods, Goddesses, Heroes, Monsters, and Other Mythical Creatures*. New York, NY: Black Dog & Leventhal Publishers, 2011.

D'Aulaire, Ingri and Edgar Parin. *D'Aulaires' Book of Norse Myths*. New York, NY: New York Review of Books, 2005.

Punter, Russell. *Usborne Illustrated Stories from the Greek Myths*. London, UK: Usborne Books, 2011.

Riordan, Rick. *The Lightning Thief: The Graphic Novel* (Percy Jackson and the Olympians, Book 1). New York, NY: Hyperion Books, 2010.

Williams, Marcia. *Greek Myths*. Somerville, MA: Candlewick Press, 2011.

Websites

Due to the changing nature of Internet links, Rosen Publishing has developed an online list of Websites related to the subject of this book. This site is updated regularly. Please use this link to access the list:

http://www.rosenlinks.com/corel/myth

INDEX